This book is dedicated to unrecognized artists of all ages
who are working hard to accomplish their dreams. —S.S.

# HOKUSAI'S DAUGHTER

## A Young Artist in Old Japan

<ruby>北斎<rt>ほくさい</rt></ruby>の<ruby>娘<rt>むすめ</rt></ruby>

### BILINGUAL **ENGLISH** AND **JAPANESE** EDITION

Story and Illustrations by

## SUNNY SEKI

サニー関
<ruby>さ に ー せき</rt></ruby>

**TUTTLE** Publishing

Tokyo | Rutland, Vermont | Singapore

Long ago in Japan, there was an artist named Hokusai. His paintings were so famous because they always had little surprises in them. His young daughter, Eijo, loved to paint too, and carried art supplies with her everywhere. She often followed her father around to watch him work.

むかし、日本の北斎という画家は、見る人を驚かすような絵で有名でした。彼の末娘、栄女も絵が好きで画材道具を持って、父のスケッチには必ず付いて行きます。

While Hokusai was drawing a tall wave, Eijo sketched a crab. Her dad said, "Your crab must be strong! Those claws are too weak to catch anything!" So Eijo drew another crab with just-right claws.

北斎は波、栄女は蟹を描いた時のこと。絵を見た父のアドバイス、「蟹はハサミが命だ。もっと強調しなさい」に、娘はうなずき、すぐ描き直しました。

4

While Hokusai taught his students, Eijo drew an elegant koi fish. "It's nice," her dad said, "but your koi needs more energy! It should be like the legendary koi who swims to the top of the waterfall to become a powerful dragon."

"I like that story," Eijo said. And she drew another koi that was lively and bold.

講習会を終えた北斎は、栄女が描いた鯉を見て「うまいがパワー不足だ。昔話で、滝を登り切った鯉は龍になるそうだよ」と教え、彼女は「わぁ、すごい話！　元気な鯉を描こう」と筆を取り直しました。

文化十四丁丑十月五日達磨半身像
東都画狂人
北齋戴斗席上

One day, Hokusai took Eijo to the city where he painted a giant portrait of Daruma. Many people gathered to watch. Hokusai splashed two blotches of ink on the paper. The crowd gasped! Had the great artist made a mistake? But Hokusai moved his brush—swish-swish-swash—and the two spots became eyes. The crowd was amazed!

"Someday I'll paint like that," Eijo thought.

巨大なダルマを描く北斎は２カ所で墨をこぼし、見物人をハラハラさせ、後で目玉に仕上げました。計略は喝采を受け、栄女は「私もいつか、皆を驚かせた～い」と胸を膨らませたのです。

The next month, Hokusai was hired to paint a hundred paper fans. It was a big job that paid him well. Eijo told the shop manager she wanted to be a painter too. But the man just laughed. "Try sewing instead, little girl!"

翌月、出版社から扇子を百枚手描きで頼まれ、北斎は大仕事にゲンナリ。でも貧乏で断れません。栄女が店員に「私も画家になりたいな」というと、「女の子は裁縫を習え」と笑われました。

Boys were even worse. "Girls can't be artists!" they said.
"Art is for boys! Look at these samurai warriors we drew!
Can a girl draw those?"

男の子たちは「女が画家になれるもんか。男の仕事だ。見ろ！
この強そうな侍を」とからかいます。

Eijo didn't answer. After they left, she drew a giant crab that grabbed the warriors in its powerful claws. The boys wanted to cover up the crab, but they were afraid that Eijo would just draw an even bigger one!

誰もいない時、栄女が蟹の怪物が侍をつまみ上げた絵を描くと、人だかりができました。男の子たちは、塗りつぶそうとしましたが、怖くなりあきらめました。

That evening, Hokusai and Eijo saw a notice announcing the birth of the Shogun's son. "This year the Boys' Day festival will be huge!" Hokusai said.

"Dad, why do people hang banners of a scary man all around the city on Boys' Day?" Eijo asked.

ある夕方、将軍に男子が生まれた掲示板が目に入り、「お祝いで端午の節供（男の子の祝日）は　賑やかになるぞ」と北斎。

「なぜ、あの怖い武者の旗を飾るの？」と栄女。

"Those are pictures of Shoki, a brave warrior who protects children. I usually paint one too. But this year I'm too busy painting fans."

Eijo became excited. "Let me paint it instead!" she exclaimed.

「あれは鐘馗という武者で子供の守護神だ。私も毎年、旗に描くが今年は扇子で忙しい」それを聞いて「じゃ、私が描こうかな」と栄女は目を輝かせました。

Hokusai wasn't sure she could do it, but he agreed to let her try. He drew a sketch of the warrior for Eijo to use as a model.

But Eijo didn't like that scary man. She had a better idea!

娘に描けるか疑いながらも、北斎はお手本を渡しました。栄女は鐘馗の怖い顔が、どうも祝日に似合わない気がします。

As her father was drawing fans and tossing away the messy ones, Eijo scooped them up.

父がポンポン投げ捨てる下絵を見ていた彼女に、素晴らしいアイデアが湧きました。

On the morning of Boys' Day, everyone was surprised to
see an immense koi fish soaring gracefully in the sky.
"Amazing!" Hokusai thought. "Eijo used my fan sketches
to make fish scales! But he was worried too. "I'm not sure if the
Shogun will like this," he thought.

端午の節供の朝、人びとは空に泳ぐ大きな鯉を見てビックリ、歓声を上げました。
北斎は「こりゃあ、驚いた。下絵がウロコになった。しかし、将軍がこんな
飾りものを許すかな」と、心配になったのです。

Soon posters of Eijo's koi could be seen all around the city. A messenger arrived from the castle to say that the Shogun wanted to meet the famous artist who had made the splendid koi.

鯉のぼりの浮世絵
ポスターが出る人気に、
江戸城から「明後日、
将軍の前で絵を描け」
と北斎に令状が来ました。

Hokusai told him the truth. "Sir, I didn't make that koi—my daughter did!"

The messenger blinked in disbelief. "Impossible! No girl can make something like that!"

On hearing this, Eijo's eyes filled with tears.

The messenger told Hokusai to come to the castle the next day, ready to paint. The Shogun wanted to see him at work.

使者に「娘が作りました」と言っても「こんな幼い女の子に出来るわけがない」と信じません。栄女は悔し涙が出てきました。

Eijo sat down with her sketchpad and dried her tears. "They say I can't be an artist because I'm a girl. Well, I'm going to show them!" And she started drawing with even more determination than before.

どうして女は画家に成れないのか、めげそうになる栄女ですが、昨日より優れた絵を描こうと毎日努力をしています。

Hokusai was nervous about meeting the Shogun. How could he impress him? Suddenly, an autumn leaf blew in the window.

"That's it!" he cried. "Eijo, come to the castle with me and bring the chicken!" For he had remembered the famous poem about red leaves on the river in autumn. He would draw the river and get the chicken to paint red leaves on it with its feet. "The Shogun will love that!" he thought.

将軍を驚かす絵を考える北斎に、紅葉が舞い込み、つられて外を見た彼は、こう叫びました。「ん！栄女、その鶏を連れて江戸城へ行こう。秋の風流は川面を流れる紅葉と歌にある。

私が川を描き、足を赤く塗った鶏を放すと足跡が紅葉に見え、将軍は美しさに大満足だ！」

Later that day, Hokusai, Eijo and the chicken appeared before the Shogun.

こうして計画通り、親子2人と鶏 1 羽は登城し、

With a swish-swish-swash of his brush,
Hokusai painted a broad, flowing river.

北斎はスイスイと流れを描き‥‥

Then, he dipped the chicken's feet in red paint and set it on the paper.

にわとり あし
鶏 の足に　たっぷり赤い絵の具を塗り、紙の上に放し
たのです。

"Everyone will be amazed when the chicken starts walking!" Eijo thought.

「さあ！足跡を見て　皆驚くぞ」と栄女も期待の一瞬！

But NO! The stubborn chicken
sat down and refused to budge!

～が、鶏は頑固に座ったまま動きません。

Everyone held their breath. What will the painter do? Hokusai himself had no idea!

But Eijo remembered how her dad had painted Daruma. She grabbed the paint bucket and rushed forward....

見物人は静まりかえり、「これは困った」と北斎が
つぶやいた時、栄女にアイデアが閃きました。
　　ダルマの目を思い出した彼女は
赤い絵の具桶をつかみ、
サッと立ちあがりました。

Swinging her arm, she splashed blotches of red paint onto the paper.

"Eijo! What are you doing?!" her dad cried out in alarm. Everyone else was stunned too!

Then Eijo began to draw lines around the blotches....

そして力一杯、紙にバチャ！　バチャ！と赤色を　ぶちまけたのです。「何をするんだ！」と北斎は真っ青、人びとは、どよめきましたが黒い輪郭を描くと・・・・

...until slowly a giant koi fish appeared!

Eijo moved her brush gracefully back and forth. The audience was filled with wonder!

"Eijo, you've saved me!" Hokusai whispered with relief.

大きな錦鯉が現れたのです！　彼女は
巧みに筆を進め、皆は感嘆の目を見開き、
北斎は「助かった！」と
胸をなでおろしました。

Hokusai added a waterfall to the painting and hung it up. "Today, I wanted the chicken to paint autumn leaves," he announced. "Instead, my daughter painted a beautiful koi! This is the famous Koi Who Climbs a Waterfall to Become a Dragon!" The crowd cheered with delight.

Eijo said to the Shogun and his wife, "Just as this koi became a dragon, so may your child become a great leader one day!"

"Yes, yes!" the Shogun cried.

水しぶきを加えた北斎は絵を松に掛け、「鯉の滝登りです。鶏が紅葉を描くはずが、娘の機転で錦鯉に化けました」と言うと暖かい笑いが起きました。

栄女が「元気な鯉は龍になるとか、お子様の無事な成長をお祈りします」と加え、将軍は「あっぱれじゃ！」と拍手で答えました。

On their way home, Hokusai told his daughter, "Eijo, I didn't realize how skillful you have become. One day you will be a great artist. Never stop believing in yourself!"

Eijo was filled with joy. "I promise I will never give up. I'm going to be just like that koi."

帰り道、「お前の絵の腕前が、こんなに上達していたとは知らなかったよ」と、北斎は心から言いました。「笑われても画家になる夢を捨てずに努力しなさい」と娘を励ましたのです。　栄女は「うん。あきらめない。滝を登る鯉の気持ち、よく分かるよ」と茶目っ気たっぷり答えました。

32

# HISTORICAL NOTES

**Katsushika Hokusai** (1760-1849), who is known by his given name, Hokusai, was a famous painter and printmaker from the Edo period. Edo was the name once used for the city that is now called Tokyo. During that time (early 1600s to the mid 1800s) prints were very popular, and it was easy for common people to buy them. The prints were made using carved blocks of wood and different colored inks. Many Japanese artists made beauiful prints, but Hokusai remains the most famous, and many artists from both East and West have been influenced by his work. Hokusai lived to age 90, and he produced over 30,000 pieces of art.

*Hokusai used himself as a model for some of his drawings. This is a drawing he made of himself in old age.*

*"Sketch of the House of Hokusai" by Tsuyuki Kosho*

**Katsushika Oei**, also called Eijo, was Hokusai's youngest child. She was an accomplished painter and is one of only a few women artists of her day to be recognized for her talent. She has become the subject of films and books, and more and more people are interested in her story and her artwork. Eijo lived with her father for most of her adult life, helping him with his work especially after he became ill.

Many believe that his later works were actually done by her. This drawing shows them at home, two artists together.

This is the first drawing by Eijo that was ever published. It was included in an anthology of poems about different provinces (which are similar to states) in Japan. The poem Eijo illustrated is about the province of Enshū (now called Shizuoka) and its

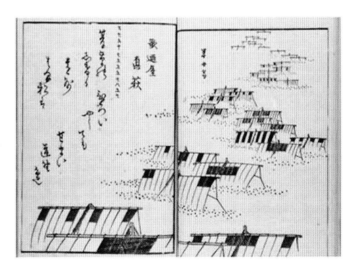

city of Hamamatsu, and the Tokaido road that stretches along its coastline. Eijo was about ten years old when she created this illustration. Because the road is by the sea, she cleverly used sails instead of people to suggest that travelers are sailing along the road. Can you find this picture on page 12?

The paintings below are among the few works known to have been painted by Eijo. Her father once said that when it comes to painting women, he couldn't compete with her. These paintings show how expert she was at capturing their expressions and movements.

*Three Women Playing Musical Instruments by Katsushika Oei, 1850 (Museum of Fine Arts, Boston)*

Eijo drew other subjects as well, and teamed up with her father on images like this one. The ancient lion inside the circle is by Hokusai; the flowers in the background were painted by Eijo (Museum of Fine Arts, Boston).

*Kinuta or Beauty Fulling Cloth in the Moonlight by Katsushika Oei (Tokyo National Museum)*

# ABOUT THE ARTWORKS IN THIS BOOK

The famous print on the left can be seen everywhere—on posters, pillows, mugs, shirts and many other things, including Japanese money and passports. If you look past the huge, crashing wave, you'll see Mount Fuji very small in the background. This print is part of a series called *Thirty-six Views of Mount Fuji*. Mount Fuji is very important and much-loved in Japan, and in each image from this series, you'll see it, sometimes in the main role and other times in the background.

Another famous image from his *Mount Fuji* series is in this book. Inside the circle of the barrel this man is making, you can see Mount Fuji in the distance. Can you find this print, and the "Great Wave" above, on page 5?

And here's another image from *Thirty-six Views of Mount Fuji*. This time, the mountain takes up the entire picture. Can you find this print on page 7?

In 1817, Hokusai used a gigantic sheet of paper to paint the Great Daruma beside a temple in Nagoya. In the painting on the left, Hokusai has painted himself with his helpers as he creates the huge portrait. Later, the Shogun – the Japanese military ruler - invited him to do a painting demonstration, and it was here that Hokusai used a chicken. We know that the Daruma painting was destroyed during a war, but there is no documentation about the fate of the chicken artwork. This fact was Sunny's inspiration to create the story in this book!

**Note:** *In the original artwork, Hokusai appears only once; the other people are not Hokusai, but his helpers. In this book, the helper is Eijo, who was probably around 17 at the time.*

Daruma, the Buddhist monk that Hokusai paints in this story, is also known as Bodhidarma. He is said to be the model for the daruma doll that has been part of Japanese culture for hundreds of years. These dolls are hollow, made mostly of paper mache, and have no limbs. They come in different sizes and may wear different colored robes, though most wear red. What they have in common is that they all start out with blank eyes. A person fills in one eye at the start of trying to achieve a goal, and fills in the other eye when that goal is reached. Daruma dolls are weighted at the bottom, so they roll and get up again – just like we need to do to achieve our goals! Have you read Sunny's other book, *Yuko-chan and the Daruma Doll*?

*Photo by Crisco 1492*

The painting attached to the story of how Hokusai used a chicken to paint fallen leaves is called *Ariwara* no *Narihira*, from the series *100 Poems by 100 Poets*. It is also called *Red Maple Leaves Floating Down the Tatsuta River*. The painting shows people fishing, swimming and crossing a bridge, but this is a close-up of the leaves on the river. What do you think—were they painted with a brush, or with chicken feet?

Did you know that Japan had manga hundreds of years ago? "Manga" is a word popularized by Hokusai to mean "comical drawing." During the nineteenth century, he created an entire book called *Hokusai Manga*, and this is one of those drawings. It tells the ancient story from India about some blind men and an elephant. Since each man was feeling a different part of the animal, each had a different idea of what it looked like.

Each was sure he was right, and, indeed, each man was a little bit right. It's a story about how important it is to remember that we all see things differently, and no one is completely right or completely wrong.

This is a wood block printing studio, where the artist, wood carver, and printer all work together. To create a woodblock print, a drawing was made on a block of wood. Everything around the drawing would be carved back so that the image would stand out, rather like a rubber stamp. One of these blocks would be carved for each color used. For a blue sky, blue ink would be applied to the sky part of the wood block and the block would be pressed onto the paper. For a flowering cherry tree, pink ink would be applied to the branches part of the block and the block would be pressed onto the paper. It took a lot of time and help to make a set of blocks, but once they were made, many copies of the same image could be printed.

*The print being produced in the studio above is "Kajikazawa in Kai Province" also called "Cormorant Fisherman" from the series Thirty-six Views of Mt. Fuji.*

*Koi Nobori Tango-no Sekku* (Boys' Day) was a festival celebrated by Samurai (noble) families on May 5th. They would display banners with *mon* (family crests) or drawings of the bold fighter Shoki to represent power. But at the end of the Edo period, the common people started to adopt *koinobori* as a new symbol. At first, all of these paper fish were black, but in 1868, when the time of the Shogun ended and power was returned to the Emperor (a time called the Meiji Restoration), families started to display different colored fish to represent all the family members, and the festival became Children's Day (*Kodomo no Hi*). Today, families fly wind socks with brightly colored koi painted on them. The koi, known for their ability to swim upstream, represent courage and determination, and the hope that children will grow and remain strong and healthy in mind, body and spirit.

*This konobori was painted by Hiroshige Utagawa, who lived at the same time as Hokusai. Typical of all early koinobori, this one is black and made out of paper. Can you find this picture in Sunny's story?*

# Books to Span the East and West

**Tuttle Publishing** was founded in 1832 in the small New England town of Rutland, Vermont [USA]. Our core values remain as strong today as they were then—to publish best-in-class books which bring people together one page at a time. In 1948, we established a publishing outpost in Japan—and Tuttle is now a leader in publishing English-language books about the arts, languages and cultures of Asia. The world has become a much smaller place today and Asia's economic and cultural influence has grown. Yet the need for meaningful dialogue and information about this diverse region has never been greater. Over the past seven decades, Tuttle has published thousands of books on subjects ranging from martial arts and paper crafts to language learning and literature—and our talented authors, illustrators, designers and photographers have won many prestigious awards. We welcome you to explore the wealth of information available on Asia at **www.tuttlepublishing.com.**

Published by Tuttle Publishing, an imprint of Periplus Editions (HK) Ltd.

**www.tuttlepublishing.com**

Library of Congress Control Number: 2024937759

ISBN 978-4-8053-1861-4

**Photo Credits**
On page 39 Top: 663highland (reproduced under the Creative Commons Attribution-Share Alike 3.0 Unported license.)
Bottom: Asturio Cantabrio (reproduced under the Creative Commons Attribution Share-Alike 4.0 International license)

**Distributed by**

**North America, Latin America & Europe**
Tuttle Publishing
364 Innovation Drive
North Clarendon, VT
05759-9436 U.S.A.
Tel: 1 (802) 773-8930; Fax: 1 (802) 773-6993
info@tuttlepublishing.com
www.tuttlepublishing.com

**Asia Pacific**
Berkeley Books Pte. Ltd.
3 Kallang Sector #04-01
Singapore 349278
Tel: (65) 6741-2178; Fax: (65) 6741-2179
inquiries@periplus.com.sg
www.tuttlepublishing.com

**Japan**
Tuttle Publishing
Yaekari Building, 3rd Floor
5-4-12 Osaki
Shinagawa-ku
Tokyo 141 0032
Tel: (81) 3 5437-0171; Fax: (81) 3 5437-0755
sales@tuttle.co.jp
www.tuttle.co.jp

First edition
28 27 26 25 24      10 9 8 7 6 5 4 3 2 1

Printed in China      2406EP

TUTTLE PUBLISHING® is a registered trademark of Tuttle Publishing, a division of Periplus Editions (HK) Ltd.

**To Download or Stream Bonus Material:**

1. You must have an Internet connection.
2. Type the URL below into your web browser.
**https://www.tuttlepublishing.com/hokusais-daughter**

For support email us at info@tuttlepublishing.com